THIS BOOK BELONGS TO

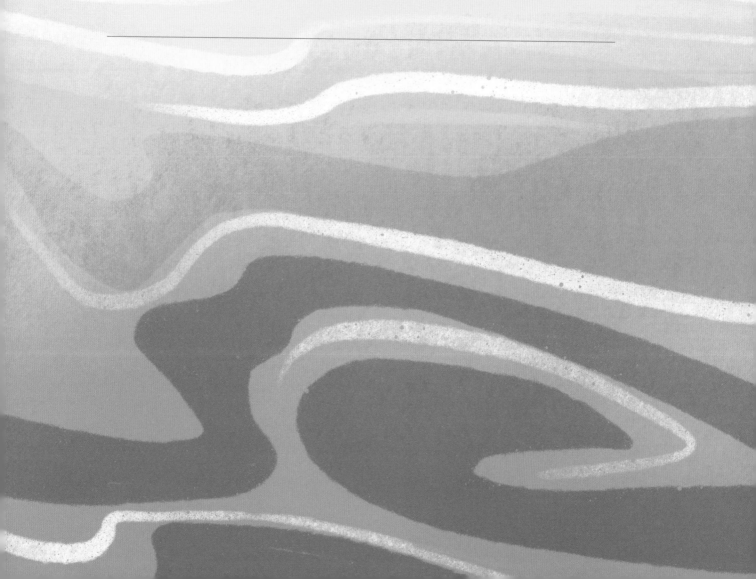

FLORIDA
FROM
A TO Z

WRITTEN BY KAREN WERNLI
ILLUSTRATED BY CHIARA CIVATI

PELICAN PUBLISHING
New Orleans

The word "Pelican" and the depiction of a pelican are trademarks of Arcadia Publishing Company Inc. and are registered in the U.S. Patent and Trademark Office.

ISBN 9781455627875

Printed in China
Published by Pelican Publishing
New Orleans, LA
www.pelicanpub.com

For Beau and Harper, and for Mom
—K. W.

Aa

**Alligator's nose is round—
he floats along without a sound.**

FIND:

acorn   airboat   airplane   alligator   ants   ant hill

Fun Florida Fact
Alligators and crocodiles have different nose shapes. An alligator's nose is round, and a crocodile's nose is pointed. Both live in the waters of Florida.

Bb

Big ocean, busy beach—
Great Blue Heron is out of reach.

FIND:

ball   blanket   blue heron   boat   boy   bucket

 **Fun Florida Fact**
A great blue heron's neck is tucked into an "S" shape when it flies, unlike a crane, which flies with its neck stretched out.

Cc

**Coreopsis scents the air—
I can smell it everywhere.**

FIND:

carousel   cat   cow   coreopsis   cotton candy   cowboy hat

Fun Florida Fact
Coreopsis is Florida's state wildflower.
Its scent is similar to licorice.

SAY: kor ee OP sis

 **Dd**

Dolphins dance, staying cool, diving in their giant pool.

FIND:

dance   dive   dog   dolphin   dress   drink

 Fun Florida Fact
Bottlenose dolphins are the most common dolphins in Florida. Winter was a famous one with a prosthetic tail! She lived in the Clearwater Marine Aquarium.

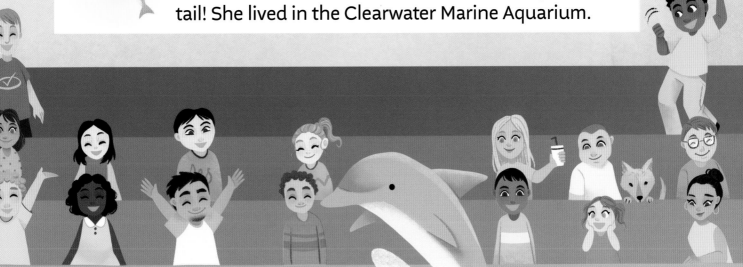

Ee

**Egrets in the Everglades—
they nest among the breezy shades.**

FIND:

eat   egg   egret   estuary

Everglades National Park   eye

Fun Florida Fact
Using their long legs, egrets wade into marshes and other waterways to hunt for their favorite meal—fish!

EVERGLADES
NATIONAL PARK

Ff

Florida Panther is out of sight, roaming the forest late at night.

FIND:

feather   Florida maple tree   Florida panther
flower   forest   fur

Fun Florida Fact
Florida panthers like to roam in the cool of the night. They can travel up to twenty miles in a day. They are Florida's state mammal.

Gg

In sunny Gulf of Mexico, Giant Grouper won't let go.

FIND:

giant grouper   girl   glasses   green   grey   gull

Fun Florida Fact
A giant grouper can weigh over eight hundred pounds! This huge fish is protected by law, so if you catch one, you must release it back into the wild.

Hh

Outside our high-rise beach hotel, we swim and find a horse conch shell.

FIND:

hammock   happy   heron   hibiscus   horse conch shell   hotel

Fun Florida Fact
Florida's state shell is the horse conch. The shell can grow to be two feet long and is home to a giant orange snail!

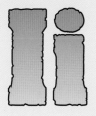

Ii

Ice cream, or Italian ice?
One each, please, they're both so nice!

FIND:

ice   ice cream   inchworm   island   Italian ice   ivy

Fun Florida Fact
There are over 4,500 islands off the coast of Florida!
The largest island is Pine Island—dolphins and
manatees swim in its surrounding waters.

Jj

Comb jellies glow on summer nights with bioluminescent lights.

FIND:

jar   jasmine   jeep   (comb) jellies   jump   June beetle

Fun Florida Fact
Bioluminescent comb jellies have existed for millions of years! Their glowing sparkles are seen in the Indian and Banana Rivers on dark summer nights.

Kk

Kiteboard shops, Key lime pie—give the Florida Keys a try!

FIND:

Key lime pie   Key lime tree   Key West map
key   kingfish   kiteboard

Fun Florida Fact
Over one thousand shipwrecks have been found in the waters of the Florida Keys!

KITE BOARDS

Ll

**Lightning flashes in the sky—
thunder rumbles its reply.**

FIND:

ladybug lake lawn leaf
lightning live oak

Fun Florida Fact
Florida is among the most lightning-struck
states in the US!

In a mangrove, thick with roots,
Great Horned Owl turns and hoots.

FIND:

manatee   mangrove   mockingbird
moon   moss   moth

Fun Florida Fact
Mangrove trees can survive in salty, or brackish, water.
Their thick, underwater root system provides safety for
many animals, including the gentle manatee.

Nn

**Nests hold eggs of many types—
snakes and turtles, loons and snipes.**

FIND:

nap   nest   night   night-blooming water lily

nine   nose

Fun Florida Fact
Different eggs have different incubation periods: six
to eight weeks for snakes, two months for sea turtles,
four weeks for loons, and three weeks for snipes.

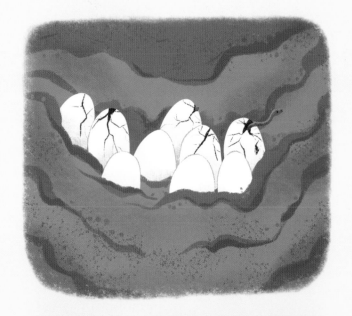

Oo

On early mornings, bright and sunny,
bees make orange blossom honey.

FIND:

"Open" sign   orange   orange blossom
orange juice   orange tree   owl

Fun Florida Fact
A ripe Florida orange can remain on the tree for several weeks—just pick what you need in the morning for a fresh glass of orange juice every day!

Orange Groves

OPEN

Pp

Waves roll in, palm trees sway— a picture-perfect weekend day.

FIND:

palm tree   people   picnic   pink
play   ponytail

Fun Florida Fact
The sabal palm is Florida's state tree. It is hard to know its age because it does not have trunk rings, but scientists believe it can live to be three hundred!

Qq

**Ducks go searching for a snack—
some stay quiet, others quack.**

FIND:

quack   quarrel   quarter   queen   quiet   quilt

Fun Florida Fact
Muscovy ducks can be identified by the bumpy, red skin on their faces. They are one of the quietest duck species in Florida. Mottled ducks, however, really like to quack!

Rr

**A red umbrella covers my head—
rain rolls onto the ground instead.**

FIND:

rabbit   rain   red   road   rock   root

Fun Florida Fact
Florida gets over fifty inches of rain each year.
It's the fourth rainiest state in the United States,
and it's the tenth sunniest!

Ss

Seashell patterns leave a trace that ocean waves will soon erase.

FIND:

sailboat   sand   seashell   sea turtle   sky   swimsuit

Fun Florida Fact
Florida has over one thousand miles of sandy coastline! Several beaches are known for having a wide variety of seashells.

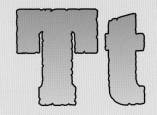

Tt

**Tourists travel, near and far—
they come by airplane, train, and car.**

FIND:

Tallahassee   Tampa   Titusville   tourists   towel   train

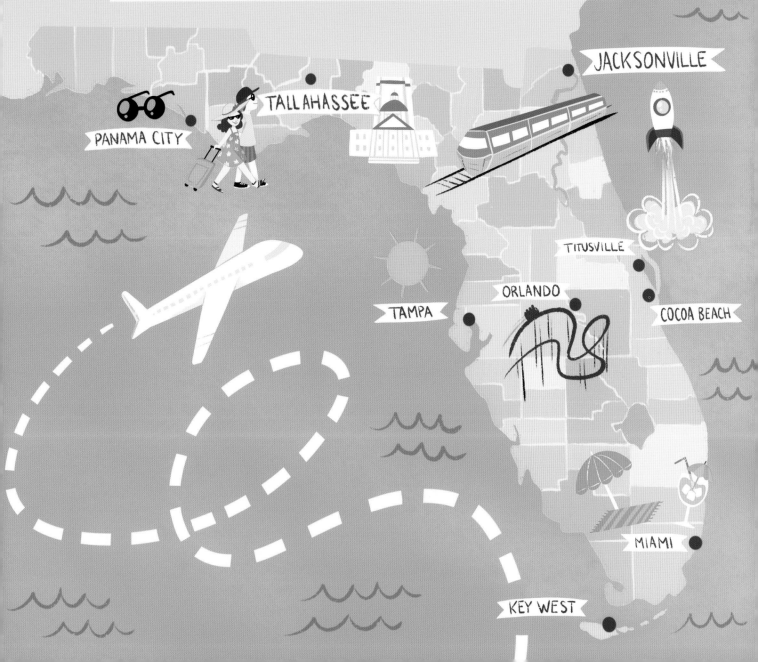

Fun Florida Fact
Florida, with its many attractions,
is one of the most popular states
for tourists!

PANAMA CITY

TALLAHASSEE

JACKSONVILLE

TITUSVILLE

ORLANDO

COCOA BEACH

TAMPA

MIAMI

KEY WEST

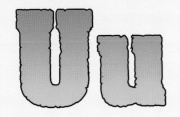

Uu

**Under the covers, under the sun,
under the stars, and now we're done.**

FIND:

under   unicorn   unicycle   uniform

United States flag   upside-down

Fun Florida Fact
Florida's nickname is the Sunshine State, and there's plenty to do under the sun!

The ocean vista's lovely hue
glows orange, pink, and violet blue.

FIND:

vegetable   vehicle   view   violet blue

visor   volleyball

Fun Florida Fact
A beach volleyball is softer, lighter, and larger than an indoor volleyball. It floats longer in the air—this is helpful because it's hard to run in sand!

Ww

Wisteria winds around a wall....
Will it wander in the hall?

FIND:

water   wave   white   window   wisteria   woman

Fun Florida Fact
Wisteria is a flowering vine—and yes, it could grow
inside the hall if the door were left open long enough!

Xx

**X-ray fish play tag in the sun—
they mix and mingle for maximum fun.**

FIND:

"EXIT" sign   Max   saxophone   taxi   XOXO   x-ray fish

Fun Florida Fact
Max has x-ray fish in his fish tank, but to find them
in the wild you would have to visit South America!

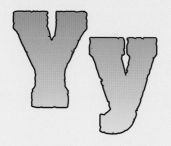

Yy

Say yes to a yacht and sail away, dangling toes in ocean spray.

FIND:

yacht   yawn   yellow   yellowfin tuna
yoga   yo-yo

Fun Florida Fact
Yellowfin tuna can swim up to fifty miles an hour! Their name comes from their bright yellow fins. They are also known as ahi tuna.

Zebra longwing butterflies zig and zag through tiger eyes.

FIND:

zebra   zebra longwing butterfly   zinnias
zip line   zipper   zoo

Fun Florida Fact
Zebra longwing butterflies are Florida's state butterfly. They live for over a month. They don't just drink nectar—they also eat pollen!

Throughout the night and every day,
the wonders of Florida are here to stay.

Florida from A to Z—

Now *you* can name
the things you see!

Florida State Symbols

 **State reptile**
Alligator

 State bird
Mockingbird

 **State butterfly**
Zebra longwing

 **State animal**
Florida panther

 **State marine mammal**
Manatee

 **State saltwater mammal**
Bottlenose dolphin

 **State flower**
Orange blossom

 **State wildflower**
Coreopsis

 **State tree**
Sabal palm

 State beverage
Orange juice

 **State shell**
Horse conch

 State nickname
The Sunshine State